MW01120624

Confrontation Management

Confrontation Management

Improve Performance and Maintain Relationships

Sam Miller

HUMBER LIBRARIES LAKESHORE CAMPUS
3199 Lakeshore Blvd West
TORONTO, ON.   M8V 1K8

ROWMAN & LITTLEFIELD
Lanham • Boulder • New York • London

Published by Rowman & Littlefield
An imprint of The Rowman & Littlefield Publishing Group, Inc.
4501 Forbes Boulevard, Suite 200, Lanham, Maryland 20706
www.rowman.com

6 Tinworth Street, London SE11 5AL

Copyright © 2019 by Sam Miller

All rights reserved. No part of this book may be reproduced in any form or by any
electronic or mechanical means, including information storage and retrieval systems,
without written permission from the publisher, except by a reviewer who may quote
passages in a review.

British Library Cataloguing in Publication Information Available

Library of Congress Cataloging-in-Publication Data

Names: Miller, Sam.
Title: Confrontation management : improve performance and maintain relationships / Sam Miller.
Description: Lanham, Maryland : Rowman & Littlefield, 2019.
Identifiers: LCCN 2018059164 | ISBN 9781475849301 (cloth : alk. paper) | ISBN 9781475849318
  (pbk. : alk. paper) | ISBN 9781475849325 (electronic)
Subjects: LCSH: School principals--Professional relationships--United States. | School administra-
  tors--Professional relationships--United States. | Teacher-administrator relationships--United
  States. | Educational leadership--United States.
Classification: LCC LB2831.92 .M56 2019 | DDC 371.2--dc23
LC record available at https://lccn.loc.gov/2018059164

♾ ™ The paper used in this publication meets the minimum requirements of American
National Standard for Information Sciences Permanence of Paper for Printed Library
Materials, ANSI/NISO Z39.48-1992.

Printed in the United States of America

Contents

Preface

Serving in a school leadership position is a privilege. School leadership is an opportunity to have significant influence, positive or negative, on the lives of students, staff, and a community.

As a young student, throughout my athletic career, I benefitted from coaches who challenged me and helped me achieve performance levels I did not think was possible. I consistently received clarity around performance strengths and areas for improvement.

After I graduated from college and became a teacher I was interested in how people in school leadership positions improved performance levels of staff members. I assumed the process would be similar to what I experienced as an athlete.

As a young teacher, observing people in leadership positions fascinated me as I was trying to figure out what type of leader I wanted to be. I was surprised and disappointed to discover that the school leaders I observed appeared to be consumed with management responsibilities and that appeared to be their primary focus.

I saw little coaching from school leaders and individual improvement was rarely, if ever, discussed.

I remember as a young teacher speaking about staff improvement with a school leader and he told me that it was too much work and the system was not designed to get rid of the bad teachers, so he instead gave the lowest-performing teachers more difficult assignments and hoped they would transfer to another school.

The school leader also told me that being a school leader had enough conflict and trouble, and a school leader did not need to create more conflict. Additionally, the message was that if he could do it all over again, he would never have become a school leader.

I remember going home and feeling dejected and demoralized. I had respected this leader and was extremely disappointed when he told me his philosophy for dealing with unsatisfactory performance and regret for becoming a school leader.

I also experienced coaching and opportunities for improvement through my personal evaluation as a teacher. As a beginning teacher, I was observed on one occasion including a post-evaluation conference.

Like most teachers, I spent countless hours preparing my lesson to demonstrate to my evaluator what a great hire I was and impress him with a quality teaching lesson.

The observation lasted thirty minutes and the post-observation conference was a checklist of activities that were observed.

My end-of-the-year evaluation was a succinct list of boxes checked "satisfactory" and I was told that I had performed at an acceptable level.

There was little feedback on areas of strength and no feedback on areas for improvement.

Suffice it to say, the process was performed to the minimum standards outlined in the master contract.

Additionally, my evaluation was not linked to a professional development plan for the following year. The evaluation process did not celebrate strengths, foster improvement, and due to the lack of feedback and coaching, the process negatively impacted my relationship with my administrator.

I was frustrated for not being recognized in the areas where I thought I was doing well and equally frustrated for the lost opportunity to have a skilled evaluator, who was invested in my development, help me improve.

As I continued my teaching journey and began taking administrative courses, I observed school leaders take different actions with low-performing teachers.

Over time, I saw a pattern in which a school leader would take one of the following actions with a staff member performing at an unsatisfactory level:

- Ignore unsatisfactory performance level
- Transfer staff to another school
- Write a positive recommendation and help the low-performing staff member get hired at another school

The eye-opening experiences I encountered early in my career impacted my focus and desire to become a different type of school leader.

I pledged to myself that when I became a school leader I would not be guilty of ignoring unsatisfactory performance, transferring a low-performing employee to another school, or signing my name to a fabricated recommendation.

I was not going to avoid having conversations about improvement, even if it meant confronting staff members about behavior or areas of unsatisfactory performance.

I have spent my entire career trying to improve my abilities as a leader to help others become the best professionals they can be.

My attempts to coach employees for improvement have included mistakes and an understanding that, upon reflection, I could have communicated performance deficits with more clarity and been more empathic in my own behavior. However, even though the process may not have been perfect, it almost always resulted in improved performance.

Through my experiences as a school leader and in professional development, feedback, and reflection, I have refined my coaching and confrontation skills.

I developed a framework that has helped me facilitate conversations that include confrontation. The confrontation framework provides a school leader with tools to plan a successful confrontational conversation.

The framework includes how to begin a conversation and commonly used tactics by employees that negatively impact a confrontational conversation.

Additionally, the framework includes guidance for a school leader on how to pivot a confrontational conversation from issues or concerns to a desired state of performance that provides clarity and examples so the employee better understands the improvement targets.

Finally, and most importantly, the framework includes how to end a confrontational conversation with intention to help maintain a positive relationship with the employee.

The Confrontation Management framework provides an employee with clarity, resources, support, and time for improvement. The framework repeatedly "invites" the employee into the conversation so they are an active participant and not simply told of the problem and the need to improve.

Most importantly, while providing all the necessary steps for improvement, the Confrontation Management framework, when implemented appropriately, does so with respect to the employee and in a manner of collaboration with the goal of maintaining a respectful relationship with the employee.

A school leader should understand that when feedback and improvement is done using the protocols in Confrontation Management, the improvement process does not happen at the expense of a trusting relationship.

One of the biggest reasons school leaders avoid confrontation is a concern for damaging or losing a positive relationship with a staff member. When implemented correctly, Confrontation Management does not damage a relationship.

In fact, when an employee is challenged to improve, and then given resources, support, and an appropriate amount of time for improvement, oftentimes improvement is achieved.

When a school leader recognizes, congratulates, and celebrates the improvement with the employee, the relationship between the school leader and the employee ends up being incredibly strong and trusting.

This book is my life's work. I hope it will help you in your journey as a leader, a coach, a mentor, and a collaborator in helping improve the education profession.

Introduction: First Coach, Then Confront

There has never been a time in the history of education that has expected, or needed, more from school leaders. There was a time when a school leader that effectively managed a school was praised and recognized by the boss.

If students were in class, instructors presented their lessons, and discipline was dealt with efficiently and decidedly, then school leaders were credited with "doing" their job.

Those days are over. Now, a school leader is expected to not only *manage* a school, but more importantly, the school leader must also effectively *lead* students and staff.

First and foremost, the leader is expected to be the lead learner of a school and co-lead with staff in ensuring that all students have an optimal learning experience.

In order to accomplish this goal, the leader must be visible throughout the school and frequently observing teaching and learning in classrooms. They must have a great understanding of the strengths and areas for improvement for each staff member.

Frequent and consistent time observing staff will not only earn the leader respect from staff for experiencing what is happening throughout the school, but also yield trust when they have individual conversations and provides customized feedback to staff members, including strengths about performance as well as areas for improvement.

A coaching conversation is a great way for a school leader to begin a relationship with staff members around performance and opportunities for improvement.

A coaching process is not evaluative; it is about observation, listening, and asking questions to help a colleague or employee gain clarity around strengths and deficit areas and then engage in collaborative conversations about improvement.

Common characteristics of an effective coaching conversation include:

• Establish trust, make the conversations safe
• Be descriptive and use data when describing strengths and deficit areas
• Ask reflective questions
• Agree on specific growth goals
• Agree on an observation schedule
• Provide timely and specific feedback
• When possible, give praise and celebrate

When a school leader uses a coaching framework, he or she has shared with an employee the need for improvement and the fact that the leader will provide support, resources, and time for improvement. An effective coaching relationship is centered on trust and the fact that the school leader and the staff member are committed to the process.

In a coaching framework, feedback is given at regularly scheduled meetings and the relationship between the school leader and the employee is much like a coach and a player. Both parties want the same outcome, which is for the staff member to be successful and improve in the identified areas.

Most school leaders are comfortable facilitating coaching conversations around improvement because it is done collaboratively with the employee and both parties view the process as improvement driven, not evaluative driven.

Because the conversation is not evaluative, it reduces conflict and stress, which results in a natural focus on improvement.

Fortunately for school leaders, most people who become educators have the personality and mindset for improvement.

Therefore, using a coaching framework is typically an effective method for a school leader to use to change employee behavior and performance level without risk of damaging the relationship.

However, what does a school leader do if a staff member is unable or unwilling to make necessary changes, and improvement is never achieved?

Furthermore, what about staff members who do not embrace feedback and are not interested in improvement? What does a leader do with an employee who does not want to be coached or see the need to be coached?

Unfortunately, every school leader will eventually have an employee that is unable or unwilling to make improvements.

A school leader may have attempted to use a coaching framework to co-own improvement with a staff member, only to discover the employee did not share the same level of concern or willingness to improve.

It is in this set of circumstances that a school leader must shift from a coaching framework to a Confrontation Management framework.

A school leader must communicate directly with an employee that the leader is changing tactics for improvement.

The leader will continue to provide additional clarity regarding employee performance deficits, continue to provide resources and support, and continue to give the employee appropriate time for improvement.

However, the school leader is shifting from a coaching process to an evaluative process to monitor employee performance.

Chapter One

Why School Leaders Avoid Confrontation

When a school leader is unsuccessful in changing employee behavior or performance through coaching conversations, the leader has two options on how to proceed.

The leader can choose to ignore the problem and think, "I tried, gave it a good effort, but the employee just wasn't able to improve."

While ignoring unsatisfactory performance is clearly not the best solution for students and the overall learning culture of a school, unfortunately it is too frequent.

To be clear, a school leader that chooses this option does so because it is easier on the school leader and the decision will result in no risk in possibly damaging a relationship or hurting the overall culture of the school.

The other option a school leader can choose when unsuccessful in using a coaching process is to confront an employee with continued concerns about behavior or performance.

While confronting an employee may seem like an easy decision, a savvy school leader understands that when they choose to confront an employee, they are not only dealing with the stress and conflict of the employee, but also the long-term relationship with the employee and the overall culture of the school.

Therefore, choosing to confront an employee can be an extremely stressful situation for both the employee and leader. The employee will likely understand that the process will result in an increased sense of urgency for improvement, and the leader will understand that they are accountable for continued feedback (which may be received as confrontational) and the fact that they will have to facilitate the process.

Confronting employees is a challenge for many people in leadership positions. School leaders have been trained on working with and sometimes confronting students, not adults.

Few people possess the skills to successfully facilitate a conversation when they need to confront an adult regarding an issue, concern, or unsatisfactory performance level.

A poorly facilitated confrontational conversation can not only result in not improving the issue or concern, which was the purpose of the conversation, but also result in damaging or ruining a relationship between a school leader and their employee.

Every time a school leader damages or loses a quality relationship with an employee it negatively impacts the overall climate of a school.

Most people who have served in a school leadership position will admit to postponing or avoiding an issue or concern if they perceived the issue to include confrontation. Confrontation is simply really difficult to facilitate and even more difficult to facilitate effectively.

There are two major reasons school leaders avoid confronting employees. The primary reason is the school leader does not believe they have the ability to successfully facilitate a conversation where an employee will receive negative feedback. Confrontational conversations can be very difficult and many people in leadership positions have not had training or professional development in how to facilitate this type of conversation.

The second and maybe more telling reason school leaders avoid confrontational conversations is because they don't want to hurt the feelings of a staff member or damage their relationship with the employee.

Every school leader wants to be liked by their staff, however some people in leadership positions choose the desire to be liked over their responsibility of ensuring all students are receiving, at a minimum, instruction by a staff member performing at a satisfactory level.

Additionally, school leaders understand that a single confrontational conversation could have bigger negative consequences than just the damage to the relationship with one staff member. A school leader understands that one negative relationship may have a negative impact on the overall culture of the school.

UNSUCCESSFULLY FACILITATING CONFRONTATIONAL CONVERSATIONS

Every person who has served in a school leadership position can look back on a conversation that included confrontation that went poorly and ended up being counter-productive. Confrontational conversations are oftentimes doomed because of three frequent problems.

One reason a confrontational conversation does not produce desired results (improved performance and maintaining a quality relationship) is because the school leader used a very authoritarian, top-down approach to the conversation.

An authoritarian (top-down) style of confrontation is when a school leader confronts an employee regarding an issue or concern, tells the employee the solution to the issue or concern, and then the consequences if the issue or concern is not fixed.

While authoritarian may sound like an appealing style to use to confront an issue or concern, in fact it may be the most problematic style for a school leader to use because it damages the relationships with the employee and can cause the most long-term damage to the culture of the school.

Sample Top-Down Conversation

Concern—staff member not dressing professionally

School leader: I called you to my office to talk with you about the way you dress. I have observed you wearing blue jeans and on some days you look more like a student than a teacher. We talked during our back-to-school workshop about appropriate dress. Professional dress is also covered in the faculty handbook. I have had other teachers complain to me about your unprofessional dress.

Employee: Who?

School leader: I am not going to share the names of the other teachers. I would appreciate you dressing in the manner that is identified in the faculty handbook. Take care of this, so I don't have to.

Employee: Part of my success with students is in the way I dress. I think students connect with me because they relate to my personality and style. I never dress sloppy or any way that would reflect poorly on this school. I don't understand why the way I dress is an issue. . . .

School leader: (Interrupting) Listen, this is not open for debate. Quit dressing unprofessionally. This does not need to be a big deal unless you make it one. I've said all I am going to say about this. Are we clear on this?

Employee: I guess.

School leader: That is all I needed, you can go back to your classroom.

A significant drawback to confronting an employee with a concern using a top-down approach is that the person in the leadership position has all the power in the conversation and that limits the effectiveness of the conversation.

In a top-down approach, an employee is never given any opportunity to "enter" the conversation.

In one-sided conversations, the emotions of the employee can escalate because of frustrations with the concern being identified and lack of power by the employee to participate or share in the discussion.

Once the temperature of the conversation rises, nobody wins.

Additionally, there is little learning that takes place when an employee is "told" of a problem and how to fix the problem.

Because there has been little participation or reflection of the employee, either the employee does not change their behavior, or the employee changes their behavior out of fear of further discipline and then *resents the school leader.*

The employee thinks the school leader is the problem, NOT their behavior.

If the employee thought his or her behavior of wearing blue jeans was a problem, they would not have engaged in the behavior in the first place.

No learning has taken place because of the intervention; YET changing behavior was the ENTIRE reason for the conversation.

A top-down approach is an efficient method to directly confronting an employee with a problem and inform the employee of the solution. However, it is not an effective strategy to change behavior while maintaining a quality relationship.

Table 1.1.   Defend, Deflect, Deny

Tactic	Definition	Example
Defend	Resist any feedback perceived to be negative, attempt to justify	"Well the reason I did that was . . ." "Everybody else is doing exactly what I am doing" "You would have done the same thing if you were in my position"
Deflect	Cause someone to change direction, deviate from intended purpose	"I understand your concern, but are you aware" (and then employee brings up unrelated topic) "I don't feel this way, but did you know that staff is really concerned about . . ." "Well, I would like to discuss . . ."
Deny	Refuse to admit, refuse to grant permission	"I don't know what you are talking about" "I didn't do that" "I don't agree with your assessment, I am never . . ."

The Hijacker

A second reason a confrontational conversation may not produce desired results is when an employee is allowed to dominate a conversation using the 3D Strategy: Defend, Deflect, Deny (see table 1.1).

Hijack Conversation

Concern—staff member repeatedly arriving late

> School leader: Thank you for stopping by my office, I hope you are having a great day. Hey, listen, I have been getting reports that occasionally you show up late for work and sometimes your class even has students in it before you arrive.

> Employee: I'll admit I have been a few minutes late recently. As many of my colleagues know, I normally am one of the first people to work, but have had a few crazy weeks, but it won't happen again.

School leader: Well, it hasn't been just this week; a few months ago, I saw you on more than one occasion pulling in the parking lot just a few minutes before first period. I meant to say something to you then but got busy.

Employee: You know how it is with little kids at home, I scramble in the morning to get them to daycare and sometimes I run a little late. It's no big deal, I am almost always in my class before students arrive, and they always get a great lesson.

School leader: You are a very good teacher and I appreciate your hard work. However, you put me in a bad position when you arrive late.

Employee: Well, I appreciate your positive comment, but I almost never miss work, so I have proven that I am committed to this school. You know there are other teachers that arrive later than I do.

I don't understand why I am getting in trouble when there are other teachers who don't come close to providing instruction like I do and yet they don't get in trouble.

School leader: What other teachers are arriving late?

Employee: Just hang out in the parking lot tomorrow morning, and you'll see the usual crew that comes in late. But you know the real issue is we have so many staff working second jobs because the salaries are so low. I think the entire staff would really appreciate it if you could help get our salaries up? I know the bargaining committee has met with you about our low wages. Are you doing anything about it?

School leader: I am not part of the bargaining group, that is done by central office. I would love it if salaries would increase. I am your biggest supporter and I don't think anybody works harder than our teachers.

Employee: Another area that needs to be addressed is class size. Do you know I have more kids on my roster this year than any other year? How can I be expected to grade so many worksheets?

Something has to be done. I know several of our substitutes that would love to work at our school and would be great. Could we discuss hiring more staff at our next faculty meeting?

School leader: I'll have to take a closer look at our roster sizes. I don't recall class size being larger this year than in past years. I'm pretty sure our enrollment is actually a little bit lower this year, and we haven't cut any teaching positions so I would be surprised if any class sizes were bigger.

Regarding hiring substitutes, they are always encouraged to apply when we have openings and some of our current faculty started out as substitute teachers. We always have hiring committees that make the decision on who is selected for teaching positions.

I don't see any reason why this should be discussed at a faculty meeting, but I would be more than happy to discuss the topic at our next building leadership team meeting.

Employee: Another thing, I don't feel this way, but are you aware that there is a rumor that staff members may complain to the board of education about your leadership?

The rest of the conversation continues with various issues from the teacher being discussed.

The school leader is unable to focus on the issue of the teacher arriving to work late, instead getting diverted by whatever diversionary issues the employee lists.

No learning has taken place because of the meeting; YET changing behavior was the ENTIRE reason for the meeting.

The school leader makes a note to avoid confronting this particular employee because it is a waste of time. The employee shares the conversation with other staff members in the school.

Eventually, the entire staff learns of the conversation and how to successfully manipulate the school leader. The school leader's reputation is tarnished due to his or her willingness to be manipulated.

The "Beats Around the Bush" School Leader

A third reason a confrontational conversation may go poorly is when the school leader lacks confidence or is uneasy about facilitating a conversation that includes confrontation.

Beats Around the Bush Conversation

Concern—teacher with classroom management issues

School leader: Thank you for stopping by my office. It is great seeing you. How is the wife and family doing? Boy, your kids are really growing up quickly; I can't believe how tall your oldest boy has gotten.

Employee: The family is doing great, thank you for asking. All the kids are growing up so quickly, and I can't believe Jonathon is already starting middle school. Where did time go so quickly?

School leader: I was in your classroom the other day and you really have it looking great. I love all the work you have done to create a fun environment for students. You have definitely gone above the call of duty.

Employee: I take pride in being a professional, and I want to thank you for noticing. I use a lot of my personal time in the evening and weekends, sacrificing time with my family so that my classroom looks great. I believe my students deserve it. Again, thank you for noticing.

School leader: Well, let's go ahead and discuss why I called this meeting. I wanted to talk with you today about your classroom management. Sometimes when I stop by your classroom, it appears that some of the students might not be paying attention. Do you ever see that, or get a sense that maybe some of the students are not as engaged in the lesson as they could be?

Employee: No, I've not really noticed that. I mean, all teachers will tell you that occasionally a student might be passively off task, and I'm sure my class is no different. But overall, I think students really like being in my classroom.

School leader: Well, I don't disagree that students like being in your class. You are one of our most popular teachers. I get a lot of requests every year from parents wanting their kid in your class. However, I do think some of the students might be taking advantage of you sometimes.

Employee: Those little rascals like to have fun; there is no doubt about it. I've discovered that if I ignore their behavior long enough, they eventually quit doing it. Last week a student went out of his way to disrupt class by playing this horrible song on his cell phone, but I just acted like I didn't hear it and the song eventually ended and then we all went back to the lesson.

School leader: You do so much for our school, I just want to make sure your classroom is as successful as everything else you do to make our school great.

Employee: I plan to volunteer again next week at the school activity. You know you can count on me. Also, I saw that we have a few new teachers, I would be more than happy to mentor one of them. I remember when I was a new teacher and how difficult it was to get the students to listen to me.

School leader: I appreciate your help, but I've already got the mentors assigned for the new staff. Anyway, is there anything I can do to help you with students so that they are more engaged in your class?

Employee: Well, now that you mention it, I would really appreciate it if you could order me a basketball hoop for my room. Not a real one, but a plastic toy version. I think the students would get a kick out of shooting hoops when they get an answer correct, or I could use it as a reward if some of the troublemakers are having a good day.

The conversation ends with the teacher not understanding the full extent of the concern by the school leader regarding classroom management. The school leader is frustrated because the teacher doesn't "get it," when in fact it was the school leader's lack of proper facilitation that caused the teacher to be confused about the purpose of the meeting.

No learning has taken place because of the meeting; YET changing behavior was the ENTIRE reason for the meeting.

Potential Results of a Poorly Facilitated Confrontational Conversation

A poorly facilitated confrontational conversation can negatively impact an entire school and negatively impact the school leader individually.

The results of a single conversation that is not well planned and facilitated can include:

Impact on Employee

- Confusion. The employee not understanding the purpose of the meeting
- The employee not feeling supported by the school leader
- The employee not embracing the feedback and no learning taking place
- The employee leaving the meeting with a negative attitude and resenting the leader
- The employee sharing with other staff members the failed conversation and telling others how to manipulate the school leader
- The employee sharing his or her negativity toward the school leader with co-workers, resulting in a more toxic school culture
- Staff realizing the leader will not confront them and the lack of accountability negatively impacting the school in multiple ways

Impact on School Leader

- The leader blaming the employee for the meeting going poorly
- The leader not improving employee performance level, so unsatisfactory performance and/or behavior is still an issue
- The leader being more hesitant to engage in a future confrontational conversation
- The leader recognizing the negative impact on school culture and working harder at getting people to like him or her
- The leader having staff challenge his or her authority and decision making

CHAPTER SUMMARY

The reasons school leaders avoid confrontational conversations:

1. School leader does not believe he or she has the ability to successfully facilitate a conversation that will include confrontation.
2. School leader is worried that a confrontational conversation will damage relationship with employee and negatively impact school culture.

The reasons for unsuccessful confrontational conversations:

1. School leader uses an authoritarian (top-down) style to facilitate the conversation.
2. Employee is allowed to hijack the meeting using the 3D Strategy (Defend, Deflect, Deny).
3. School leader uses a "Beat Around the Bush" style to facilitate the conversation.

The results of poorly facilitated confrontational conversations:

1. Confusion by the employee and blame by school leader
2. No learning taking place; employee resenting school leader and damaging long-term relationship
3. Employee sharing conversation with other staff members, which negatively impacts school culture
4. Staff learning how to manipulate the school leader
5. Employee sharing with other staff members how to manipulate school leader
6. Reduced accountability
7. Leader less likely to engage in confrontational conversations
8. Staff challenges school leader authority and decision making

Chapter Two

Confrontation Management

This chapter will focus on a framework to help a school leader plan a confrontational conversation.

There are five steps to planning a confrontational conversation using the Confrontation Management framework. Each step includes specific planning details that are critically important for the overall success when a school leader facilitates a confrontational conversation. (A Confrontation Management Template is included in chapter 8.)

STEP 1. STATING THE PROBLEM

A common problem with confrontational conversations is the school leader not knowing how to begin the meeting. It is natural for a school leader to be nervous when facilitating a confrontational conversation.

Nervousness or wanting to delay confrontation can result in the school leader fumbling at the beginning of a meeting, which can set the stage for a confusing meeting for the employee.

Common mistakes in beginning a confrontational conversation include:

- Lack of clarity in opening statement resulting in the employee not understanding the reason for the meeting.
- Including judgment in an opening statement ("I am really disappointed in you").
- A lot of small talk that wastes time and minimizes the purpose of the meeting (see chapter 1, "Beats Around the Bush").
- The school leader giving compliments to the employee and then getting to the main issue, which is a concern. From the employee's perspective, the compliments may outweigh the concern, so they walk away feeling supported by the school leader and not understanding the need to improve.
- Beginning a conversation by asking the employee a question about a concern that results in the employee answering the question from the employee's perspective, which typically is not an accurate depiction of the problem. Sets the meeting up as a "debate" on which perspective is more accurate.

With Confrontation Management, the person in the leadership position begins the conversation by welcoming the employee and then stating the problem. The opening statement is simple and provides clarity to the employee.

Leadership Memo

The school leader should keep the focus of a confrontational conversation to a single problem. It is important for the school leader to avoid bundling multiple issues or concerns with the employee. A leader may have an employee with several deficit areas, however the recommended strategy is to focus on the main issue or concern only. Additional concerns can be addressed at a future meeting. (KISS: Keep It Simple Stupid.)

Examples of effective opening statements include:

Example 1

Good morning Ms. Taylor. I asked to meet with you because I want to discuss your frequent use of a cell phone during instruction time. I have witnessed this behavior on multiple occasions and during instruction time, your focus should be on students.

Example 2

Good afternoon Mr. Jones, I want to talk with you today about your classroom management. I have spoken with you previously about the number of students that are frequently not engaged in your lesson, but unfortunately, I have not observed any improvement. At our meeting today we are going to discuss this issue in detail and identify a plan for improvement.

Example 3

Thank you, Mr. Smith, for meeting today. I want to discuss the school not being cleaned at an acceptable level. You and I have discussed this issue in the past and as the lead custodian, this must be improved immediately. We are going to discuss in detail the specific issues and identify a plan for improvement.

In each of the sample statements, the issue is brought to the employee's attention with clarity and (in some cases), includes the fact that an improvement plan will be part of the meeting.

STEP 2. INVITING THE EMPLOYEE INTO THE CONVERSATION

Once a school leader has shared a concern in the opening statement, the employee is invited into the conversation as the school leader asked them to share their thoughts.

It is important to get an employee talking early in the meeting so they are an active participant throughout the conversation. Therefore, as soon as the school leader has presented the concern, the employee should be "invited" into the conversation to share their perspective.

Sample Opening Statement Inviting the Employee into the Conversation

The sample opening statement from example #1 will be used again, but additional phrasing has been added inviting the employee into the conversation:

Good morning Ms. Taylor. I asked you to my office because I want to discuss your frequent use of a cell phone during instruction time. I have witnessed this behavior on multiple occasions and during instruction time, your focus should be on students. *As you hear the concern about your cell phone use during instruction time, what are your thoughts?*

A school leader should be prepared that when an employee is invited into the conversation they may try to use the 3D Strategy, Defend, Deflect, Deny (chapter 1, table 1.1).

If the employee attempts to take the conversation in any direction away from the main problem presented by the school leader, the leader must be prepared to state, "I am more than happy to discuss those issues at a separate meeting, today we are discussing" (restate the problem).

Another option for a school leader is to thank the employee for sharing a concern, however, state that the focus of the meeting today is (restate the problem).

In chapter 1 an example of a Hijack Conversation was provided. This is a frequent strategy that employees use to avoid talking about unsatisfactory performance level or behavior.

The employee will use another staff member's behavior or unsatisfactory performance, school rumors, or other means of distraction to get a school leader to focus on anything other than the employee's behavior or unsatisfactory performance.

It is not uncommon for an employee who feels threatened by a confrontational conversation to try to switch the focus of the conversation to the school leader's behavior or performance.

Employees will use phrases like, "I don't feel this way, but did you know" and then create a scenario with the hopes of the school leader then defending against the allegation.

Another tactic employees use, "Are you aware that staff is upset with you" and then create a real or fictional reason why staff may be upset with the school leader.

If at any time in a confrontational conversation an employee tries diversionary tactics, the school leader must be prepared to either ignore the comment or make a statement getting back to the problem. *This strategy cannot be emphasized enough.*

A common mistake for school leaders is "taking the diversionary bait" from an employee and wasting significant time on a different and possibly non-existent problem.

When a school leader allows the focus of a confrontational conversation to be switched or delayed it will result in reducing the effectiveness of the confrontational conversation.

Monitoring Time

The school leader must be intentional to not dwell too long on an unsatisfactory performance issue of an employee. The leader should state the problem and allow the employee to share their thoughts.

The leader should be prepared to give examples of the problem if needed, but after adequate time has been given to ensure the employee understands the problem and the need to improve, the leader should then direct the conversation to the next phase of Confrontation Management—The Pivot.

STEP 3. THE PIVOT

After sufficient time and examples have been given regarding the issue or concern, the leader will now pivot the conversation to desired outcomes.

A sample pivot statement: "We have discussed the area for improvement, now let's discuss in detail how your actions/behavior will look differently in the future. I am confident that together we can help you improve in this area."

The leader will describe the desired outcomes with as much clarity as possible. It is critical that the school leader describes and defines the desired outcome, not the employee. By having the leader describe the desired outcome, there should be clarity around what performance should look like.

Once the leader has described the desired outcome, the leader will ask the employee for their thoughts about the desired outcome. Again, this is reinforcing the need for the employee to be an active participant in the conversation.

A sample statement for the school leader would include: "As you hear me describe what your performance should look like, what questions do you have?"

Leadership Memo

Desired outcome(s) is not open for debate. The leader is simply trying to make sure both the school leader and the employee are clear about future expectations.

The leader may want to ensure understanding by asking a few clarifying questions regarding the desired state to make sure the employee is clear on expectations.

If at any time the employee appears confused or does not understand the desired state as described by the school leader, the school leader should be prepared to provide additional details and share examples of how the behavior or performance should look and, equally important, how it should not look. It may be advisable to schedule an observation of a colleague where the school leader and teacher can clearly see the teacher behavior or action being demonstrated at a satisfactory or exceeding level.

It is during this phase of Confrontation Management where the real learning takes place for the employee in the conversation. In this stage in the meeting, a leader may learn why an employee has failed to demonstrate certain behaviors or other factors that negatively impact performance.

If an employee wants to continue to debate the desired outcome (they either disagree about their performance level or the ability to meet the desired outcome), the leader has a couple of options on how to proceed.

There are two examples below on how a school leader can proceed. The first example is a "softer" or gentler approach a school leader can use with an employee who may be a little confused and does not quite grasp the purpose of the conversation.

The second approach is a firmer, authoritarian approach and should be used with an employee who is mad, defiant, or lacks a sense of urgency for improvement.

A softer approach:

"I am so glad we are having this conversation, as I am better understanding how we are not aligned in our vision. (Restate the employee's name), I need you to meet my expectation. I know you can do it, but I need to be very clear, this has to improve."

A firmer approach:

"The desired outcome is what I need from you. If you cannot meet this expectation, we may need to have a different conversation about your future employment with this organization. You need to tell me how to proceed."

This will give the employee the power to decide how the conversation will proceed. If the employee is unwilling or unable to meet the desired outcome, the leader should discuss alternative options, most likely including a letter of resignation.

If the employee agrees to the desired outcome, then the leader and the employee talk about resources and support to help the employee improve performance. A skilled facilitator will show the utmost respect and support for the employee to convey their commitment to helping the employee make the necessary improvement.

By having the employee identify actions and behaviors to remedy the situation, the leader has shifted from telling the employee solutions to agreeing with the employee on solutions.

Sample Desired Outcome

The opening statement example #1 from earlier in this chapter will be used as an example for a desired outcome.

Opening Statement

Good morning Ms. Taylor. I asked to meet with you because I want to discuss your frequent use of a cell phone during instruction time. I have witnessed this behavior on multiple occasions during instruction time, your focus should be on students.

Desired Outcome

School Leader

"I want to make sure we are both on the same page with future expectations regarding cell phone usage during instruction time. We have both agreed that your cell phone should not be used during instruction time.

Your cell phone should be put away and there should be no phone conversations, texting, or any other use of the cell phone. Use of your cell phone during instruction time would be a violation of my expectation. Do you have any questions about how I have described the desired outcome?

As a reminder, I will put this agreement in writing within the next couple days and we will both sign copies of the agreement and each keep a copy."

STEP 4. IDENTIFYING A PLAN AND DOCUMENTING THE CONVERSATION

The primary goal of Confrontation Management is to engage an employee in a conversation with the purpose of improvement while maintaining a quality relationship. A secondary goal is to put the employee on notice regarding his or her area of concern as well as a plan for improvement.

A school leader may go into a conversation with a strong coaching intent, however, inevitably, a school leader will experience an employee who is unwilling or unable to make improvements and therefore documenting the meeting where performance deficits were addressed and an improvement plan was discussed and developed may prove beneficial if termination later becomes necessary.

After the school leader and employee have agreed to a verbal description of the desired outcome and the resources and support to help them achieve success, the school leader should tell the employee that they will capture the content of their meeting and develop a written plan that they can both review and sign in the next few days.

This will provide the school leader time to develop a plan, identify all components discussed with the employee, and include regularly scheduled meetings to discuss progress.

When possible, the school leader and Human Resource Director should review and jointly approve the improvement plan prior to sharing with the employee.

When the improvement plan is presented to the employee, the school leader should use language including, "I believe I captured our conversation and everything we agreed to. Please review and then let's discuss it in detail." This will help both parties know exactly what to expect and commitments by both parties.

Stating the plan in this manner will also reinforce that the improvement plan development was a collaborative effort.

At the bottom of the improvement plan, the school leader should make sure both parties sign and date two copies of the document, one for the supervisor and one for the employee.

The improvement plan will be an active document that should be referenced throughout the terms of the plan. Additionally, the improvement plan will serve as an artifact if the employee is unsuccessful in making improvements as outlined in the plan.

Leadership Memo

The school leader must follow the improvement plan EXACTLY as written. Failure by the school leader to provide support or facilitate review meetings as specified in the plan will reduce the likelihood of success and send a message that the school leader is unwilling to provide agreed-upon support.

Additionally, failure to comply with the terms of the improvement plan will render the improvement plan useless as an artifact for management in a termination proceeding and actually help the employee by showing that management did not follow the plan as written.

Nothing looks worse in a hearing than a school leader who has failed to do the actions in a plan that they wrote.

STEP 5. ENDING THE CONVERSATION

After the school leader and the employee have agreed to desired outcomes and the terms of an improvement plan, the leader needs to end the conversation strategically. There are two parts to end a conversation using the Confrontation Management framework.

Part I—Agree on What Leaves the Meeting

This first step in ending a confrontational conversation using the Confrontation Management protocols is an agreement between the school leader and the employee on keeping private the conversation and everything that was discussed between the two parties. However, a school leader only controls 50 percent of the power in keeping the conversation private.

A disgruntled employee can hurt the culture of a school if they exit a confrontational conversation and start complaining to colleagues about unfair treatment by the school leader.

Therefore, a leader needs to address what, if anything, will be shared with other staff members. A sample statement for a school leader includes, "Do you think any other staff members need to know about this conversation?"

This will give the employee the power to decide what is shared or not shared. Most employees will not want any other employees to know that the school leader met with the employee privately to discuss a concern.

The school leader can validate the need to keep the conversation private by saying, "I agree, nobody needs to know about this conversation and I definitely will not be sharing it with anybody."

Implicit in the statement is the fact that if staff members learn of the conversation, both the school leader and the employee will know whom the leaker was.

However, if the employee chose to share the conversation, or the concern happened in public, strict confidentiality may not be possible. In these occasions, the leader and the employee have to agree to exactly what is to be shared and how it will be shared, including actual statements.

Leadership Memo

Agreeing to what will be shared with staff is done so the staff member is coached on how to share the issues or concerns discussed during the confrontational conversation appropriately. A school leader should NEVER share a private conversation with staff.

If a school leader has concerns that the employee may violate keeping a conversation private, the school leader must decide if sharing the conversation with other staff members would warrant additional discipline.

In some cases, an entire staff knowing about a confrontational conversation may provide notice to other staff that may also be struggling with the same issue or concern.

However, in other cases, it may cause the school leader additional problems if a concern is shared and may require the school leader to meet again with the employee. If additional discipline would occur, the school leader must share the potential ramifications in advance with the employee.

Part II — Acknowledgment and Validation

The final step to end a conversation using the Confrontation Management framework is for the leader to validate the employee for their professionalism and positive characteristics and thank the employee for how they contribute to the school and make it successful for students.

The school leader should reiterate their pledge to help the employee make necessary improvements. Ending the conversation on a positive note will positively impact the long-term relationship with the employee and help the overall culture of the school.

Sample Acknowledgment and Validation

"I want to thank you for meeting today and the professionalism you modeled throughout our conversation. I value you and am committed to doing whatever I can to help you. You are a leader in this school and, as you know, somebody that I depend on. I know you are busy so I'll let you get back to your busy schedule, but remember, please do not hesitate to ask if there is anything I can do to help and support you."

CHAPTER SUMMARY

Confrontation Management Protocols

Step 1: *State the Problem*

The opening statement is simple, direct, and one issue that provides clarity to the employee. KISS (Keep It Simple Stupid.)

Step 2: *Invite the Employee into the Conversation*

Once a school leader has shared the concern in the opening statement, the employee is invited into the conversation by asking them to share their thoughts. Be aware, the employee may try to use the 3D strategy (Defend, Deflect, Deny).

Monitoring Time

The leader must be intentional to not dwell too long on the problem. State the problem, allow the employee time to share their thoughts, but after enough time has been given to ensure the employee understands the problem and the need to improve, then move on to the next phase of the conversation.

Step 3: *The Pivot*

After sufficient time and examples have been given regarding the problem, the leader will now pivot the conversation to desired outcomes. Desired outcome(s) is not open for debate. The leader is making sure both parties (school leader and employee) have a clear understanding of future expectations.

If an employee wants to debate the desired outcome, the leader has two options to proceed.

The Softer Approach

The softer approach is used when an employee may be a little confused and does not quite grasp the purpose of the conversation, but the school leader believes the employee has the attitude, desire, and sense of urgency to improve.

The Firmer Approach

The firmer approach is used when, as a result of bringing a concern to the attention of an employee, the employee becomes mad, defiant, or lacks a sense of urgency for improvement.

Step 4: *Identifying an Improvement Plan and Documenting the Conversation*

After the school leader and employee have agreed to a verbal description of the desired outcome and the resources and support to help them achieve success, the school leader should inform the employee that they will be meeting again in the near future to review a written plan.

Step 5: *Ending the Conversation*

The leader needs to end the conversation strategically.

Part I—Agree on What Leaves the Meeting

A school leader needs to address what, if anything, from the conversation will be shared with other staff members.

Part II—Acknowledgment and Validation

The final step to end a conversation is for the leader to validate the employee for positive characteristics and thank the employee for how they contribute to the school and make it successful for students.

Following the steps used in Confrontation Management will increase the likelihood for a successful conversation.

If an employee has clarity, support, resources, and time, oftentimes the employee is able to make necessary improvements.

When an employee is able to make improvement, then the leader is able to celebrate the improvement with the employee, which is described later in the book.

Chapter Three

Facilitating Confrontation Management

The previous chapter focused on using the Confrontation Management framework to *plan* a confrontational conversation. Chapter 3 will focus on how to use the Confrontation Management framework to successfully *facilitate* a confrontational conversation.

Many school leaders have scar tissue from facilitating a confrontational conversation without a plan that did not go well.

It may sound like common sense but planning out a confrontational conversation provides a school leader with a detailed plan for the many variables that can happen with that type of meeting. Planning for a confrontational conversation also provides the school leader with more confidence going into the meeting.

Several key considerations are helpful in facilitating a successfully planned confrontational conversation. In the following pages, the five-step plan will be described in detail.

1. SCHEDULING THE MEETING

A school leader should be very considerate of an employee's schedule when identifying a time for a meeting.

The school leader must find a time that will provide both parties with an appropriate amount of time to meet, so that the conversation is not rushed because one of the participants has another commitment.

A school leader will discover that if some employees know the content of an upcoming confrontational conversation (for example, if the initial meeting is not able to be completed), then the employee is more prepared and armed to defend current practice or deflect the conversation and the meeting can become much more difficult to facilitate. Therefore, a school leader should complete the conversation in one meeting.

A school leader should avoid scheduling a confrontational conversation at a time that is convenient for him or her but does not take into consideration the employee's schedule or responsibilities. If, for example, an employee has an extra duty or only a short break, then the school leader should find an alternative time to schedule the meeting.

Although seasoned school leaders consistently use Friday afternoon to give bad news in order to lessen the impact on gossip and negatively impacting school culture, scheduling a confrontational conversation on Friday at 4:00 is not conducive to changing behavior and improving performance. The employee will say whatever it takes so they can leave the meeting and begin their weekend.

A school leader should schedule a confrontational conversation with an employee when the staff member has, at a minimum, at least a thirty-minute opening in their schedule.

A school leader typically knows his or her staff members well enough and understands that some employees may require more time to process and communicate in a sensitive conversation.

If an employee's schedule does not include a break with adequate time for a meeting, then the school leader should meet the employee at the beginning or end of a work day.

The leader should be prepared for an employee who may not be able to meet on the same day that the employee is given notice of the need to meet. Additionally, a school leader should give the employee multiple options on when to meet so the employee can pick a time that is more convenient for them.

2. MEETING NOTIFICATION

Email is an easy way to notify an employee about a need to meet, but it may not be the best way to communicate the need to meet.

The school leader should keep in mind that improving performance is one goal of scheduling a confrontational conversation; however, maintaining a positive, trusting relationship is another goal.

How a leader chooses to notify a staff member is one of many choices made by a school leader throughout a process that includes a confrontational conversation that will ultimately impact a relationship between a school leader and a staff member.

3. MEETING NOTIFICATION VS. ACTUAL MEETING

Nobody likes to be told by their boss that they want to meet. The more time that passes between a meeting notification and the actual meeting will cause most people significant stress.

Human nature is for people to be worried when their boss wants to meet. People tend to let their insecurities get the best of them and it is not uncommon for people to begin thinking worst case scenarios and wondering if they did something wrong or if they are going to get fired.

If a school leader wants to keep an employee's stress and anxiety at a minimum, they should reduce the time between meeting notification and the actual meeting.

A. Notify and Meet

When considering a meeting using Confrontation Management framework, if a school leader does not have any concerns about the attitude or mindset of an employee, the leader should use a Notify and Meet tactic.

With Notify and Meet, the school leader will have already planned for the meeting using the Confrontation Management framework and then seek out the employee a time when they know the employee has an appropriate amount of time to meet. With this tactic, the employee is told of the need to meet AND given the opportunity to meet at that time. Most employees will appreciate this tactic as it eliminates time to worry about the meeting.

B. Notify and Wait

If a school leader is concerned about an employee's negative attitude or lack of urgency regarding improvement, then the leader can intentionally notify the employee of the need to meet and then not schedule the meeting until at least one day later.

The time between the meeting notification and the actual meeting will create time for the employee to think about why their boss has scheduled a meeting. As was mentioned earlier, most people will experience stress over what might occur during the meeting.

When using the Notify and Wait tactic, the leader must be prepared for the employee to ask, either in person or by written communication, what the meeting is regarding.

The leader should state that they want to discuss the employee's performance level. If the employee persists and wants more details, the leader should state that additional details will be shared at the meeting.

Leadership Memo

A leader should be prepared for an employee asking whether they should have a representative of the Association (Union or Bargaining Committee) to accompany them to the meeting. A leader should never attempt to dissuade an employee from having representation at a meeting when performance is being discussed. A sample response to questions around union representation at the meeting could include:

School Leader

You are more than welcome to have a member of the Association join you at the meeting if that would make you feel more comfortable. We will be discussing performance deficits and I will provide clarity on areas for improvement. You are certainly welcome to have representation from the Association observe the conversation.

4. MEETING LOCATION

Meeting in a school leader's office is not always the best location to host a confrontational conversation. Nobody, not even adult staff members, likes getting called to the boss' office.

If possible, a school leader should pick a neutral location, like a conference room, to have the meeting. If possible, a great place to meet is in the employee's classroom or workspace. Scheduling a confrontational conversation in an employee's classroom or workspace will provide the employee with a comfortable environment and help lower their stress and anxiety during the meeting.

The meeting location should provide appropriate privacy and the employee should not feel they are "on display" for other staff members to see them meeting with the school leader.

5. SITTING STRATEGICALLY

When the school leader arrives for the meeting, they should pull up a student desk or sit in a manner that the employee and school leader are at the same eye level.

Standing or sitting in a position that requires the school leader to "look down" at the employee is not only symbolically wrong, but it will reduce the effectiveness of the conversation.

Additionally, the leader needs to sit where they will not be distracted during the meeting. For some school leaders, it is recommended they put away their cell phone so they resist the distraction of text messages, phone calls, or email notifications.

It is imperative that when the employee speaks, the school leader is listening, making eye contact, and modeling appropriate body language.

The employee should feel that the school leader is engaged in the conversation and does not pick up on any unintended signals that the leader is distracted, not listening, or appears to have already made up his or her mind.

CHAPTER SUMMARY

Several key considerations are helpful in executing a successfully planned confrontation management conversation, including:

Step 1: *Scheduling the Meeting*

The school leader should identify a time for a confrontation meeting that will provide the leader with the appropriate amount of time to facilitate the Confrontation Management framework and the conversation is not rushed because one of the participants has another commitment.

Step 2: *Meeting Notification*

A leader should consider the most appropriate manner in which to notify an employee of the need to meet. While email is efficient, it may not be the most effective method.

Step 3: *Meeting Notification vs. Actual Meeting*

Notify and Meet

In this scenario, the employee is told of the need to meet AND given the opportunity to meet at that time, that is, there is no delay in meeting.

Notify and Wait

If a school leader is concerned about an employee's negative attitude or lack of urgency regarding improvement, then the leader can consider intentionally notifying the employee of the need to meet and then not schedule the meeting until at least one day later.

Step 4: *Meeting Locations*

A school leader should be intentional when picking the location for a meeting that will involve confrontation. The leader should pick a location that will provide privacy and not result in the employee feeling they are "on display" for people to judge. If possible, the leader should consider meeting in the employee's classroom or workspace.

Step 5: *Sitting Strategically*

When the school leader arrives for the meeting, they should pull up a student desk or sit in a manner that the employee and school leader are at the same eye level.

A leader may want to put their cell phone away to avoid distractions.

Chapter Four

Follow Up and Celebration

Many people who choose to be an educator have a mindset for excellence. Therefore, when an educator is given feedback regarding deficits in their performance, even when the feedback is done by the most gifted facilitator of a confrontational conversation, the news will likely cause stress and disappointment with an employee.

Hearing negative feedback about your performance is difficult for most people.

A critical step of effective Confrontation Management implementation is what the school leader does *after* a confrontational conversation.

A confrontational conversation is focused on areas of improvement for an employee. However, the immediate action a leader takes with an employee following the confrontational conversation is focused on the continued trusting relationship with the employee.

As was cited in chapter 2, the final step to end a conversation using the Confrontation Management framework is for the leader to validate the employee for positive characteristics and thank the employee for their positive contributions to students and the school.

The actions and behavior of the school leader following a confrontational conversation are intended to build on the positive comments shared by the school leader at the end of the confrontational conversation.

Within forty-eight hours after facilitating a confrontational conversation, the school leader should intentionally seek out the employee and have a social interaction. The conversation between the school leader and the employee should focus on positive aspects of the relationship between the school leader and the employee.

The follow up conversation should *not* include any concerns discussed during the confrontational conversation.

The follow-up conversation is intended to be a positive interaction and the school leader should use natural talking points like family, vacations, and known interests of the employee.

The sole purpose of the follow-up conversation is for the school leader and the employee to return to their natural interactions and not let the confrontational conversation become an impediment to the relationship between the school leader and the employee.

A school leader should monitor the employee's visibility and communication.

If the school leader senses any red flags, like the employee staying in their classroom or workspace, avoiding the school leader or colleagues, staying out of the main office, or other behaviors that are abnormal, the school leader should seek out the employee and facilitate a conversation to try and rebuild the relationship.

A leader that ignores a lack of visibility or other negative behaviors of an employee that has recently participated in a confrontational conversation runs the risk of permanently losing a positive relationship with the employee.

An upset employee will most likely share his or her negative attitude with colleagues and behave in a manner that hurts the culture of the school.

A school leader should try to have a positive relationship with every staff member. A leader cannot afford to lose a positive relationship every time the leader facilitates a conversation that includes confrontation.

CELEBRATION

Quality school leaders understand the importance of celebrating students and staff members. These leaders identify and create opportunities to make people feel special and are intentional about the various tactics they use to promote a positive culture.

Unfortunately, some school leaders do a poor job celebrating good news with staff. The demands of a school leadership position are daunting, and some leaders miss opportunities for celebration.

While it may seem counterintuitive, a confrontational conversation is a potential opportunity for celebration. If an employee who participated in a confrontational conversation begins making improvements in performance, the school leader should celebrate the improvement.

One simple, yet powerful way to celebrate a staff member is a short, hand-written note. This is a particularly effective way for a school leader to show appreciation. It is not uncommon for teachers to proudly display hand-written notes from their school leader.

For some employees, public praise is the most powerful manner in which they can be recognized.

A skilled school leader can take what was once a concern with an employee and turn it into an opportunity to develop a trusting relationship with a colleague that will result in mutual respect and loyalty.

Leadership Memo

In a personal, hand-written note, praise the improvement without mentioning concerns or the improvement plan.

Regarding public praise, a school leader should consider the employee's personality and understand that some people do not like to be recognized in public. When in doubt, a school leader should ask the employee for permission to recognize the employee in front of their colleagues.

CHAPTER SUMMARY

Within forty-eight hours of facilitating a confrontational conversation, the school leader should intentionally seek out the employee and have a follow-up conversation that should focus on positive aspects of the relationship.

The follow-up conversation is intended to be a positive interaction and the school leader should use natural talking points like family, vacations, and known interests of the employee.

School leaders need to celebrate students and staff. Improvement from a confrontational conversation is an excellent opportunity to celebrate the employee. The leader should consider whether private or public praise is the preferred method by the employee.

Chapter Five

Practicing Confrontation Management

For many people, confrontation is not a natural or comfortable way to communicate. Most school leaders will readily admit that their administrative preparatory program did not include instruction on how to facilitate a confrontational conversation.

So how does a school leader improve their ability to appropriately confront employees?

More importantly, how does a school leader improve their ability to appropriately confront employees AND maintain a trusting relationship?

The best way to improve in facilitation of a confrontational conversation is to practice. There are several different ways a school leader can practice Confrontation Management protocols including:

ROLE PLAYING

Role playing is a great method for school leaders to practice their facilitation skills and become more comfortable engaging in a conversation that includes confrontation.

With role playing, the school leader identifies a colleague to play the role of an employee. The school leader describes a scenario and tells the colleague about an issue on which he or she will be practicing their Confrontation Management skills. The leader gives the colleague permission to behave in a manner consistent with an upset employee and to discuss issues and concerns an employee might say in a confrontational meeting.

The colleague should challenge the school leader by improvising statements to help the school leader be more prepared for multiple scenarios with the employee. Having the person playing the role of the employee make various statements designed to deflect a conversation is an excellent way to improve a school leader's skill at ignoring deflecting comments and redirecting a confrontational conversation back to the main issue or concern.

The school leader should use the confrontation management template to plan the conversation.

THIRD-PARTY COACH

Another method to practice Confrontation Management protocols is for a school leader to invite a third-party coach to observe a role-playing practice session and provide feedback on strengths and areas for improvement.

By using a coach who is not participating in the confrontational conversation, they can focus on behavior and actions of the school leader and identify whether the school leader has any nervous habits or other non-verbal communications that reduce the effectiveness of the conversation.

VIDEO RECORDING

Video recording practice sessions is another way for a school leader to practice their facilitation skills. Like with a third-party coach, recording practice facilitation sessions allows a school leader to look for speech pattern habits, overuse of particular words or phrases, and inadvertent gestures that positively or negatively impact the effectiveness of the conversation.

PRACTICE SCENARIOS

Multiple scenarios have been included for a school leader to practice their confrontational conversations facilitation skills. Each sample scenario includes the issue or concern for the school leader, as well as a "script" for the person playing the role of the employee.

The person playing the role of the employee is given comments to read during the practice session. The purpose of providing the comments for the employee is to create a realistic depiction of what an actual confrontational conversation would look like.

Also, by providing the person playing the role of the employee and giving them the 3D Strategy (Defend, Deflect, and Deny—see chapter 1), the person playing the role of the employee will better prepare the school leader for the various tactics used during a confrontational conversation.

Scenario 1

Role of School Leader

You are meeting with a teacher who has a reputation for kicking students out of his class. However, in recent weeks, the teacher has significantly increased the number of students removed from class. You have voiced your concern with this employee in the past, but now feel you need to address the concern and develop an improvement plan.

Role of the Employee

You are a teacher who routinely kicks students out of class. The school leader has requested a meeting and you assume your kicking students out of class will be the topic.

1. As the school leader brings the concern to your attention, you state, "You have got to be kidding me. You know I run a tight

ship, and my test scores are annually some of the best in this school."

2. Later in the meeting, you state, "The real issue is that students get sent to the office but there is no punishment. That is why students think getting sent to the office is such a joke.

3. Toward the end of the meeting, you say, "Listen, I respect your authority, but I am struggling with this meeting. I may need to go above your head to get this taken care of."

Scenario 2

Role of the School Leader

You are meeting with a teacher who leaves her class unsupervised for various reasons like making copies, going to the restroom, or getting something from a neighboring teacher. Earlier in the year a fight broke out during unsupervised time and you spoke with the teacher about the problem. Now, you feel an improvement plan is needed due to another student safety concern.

Role of the Employee

You are a teacher and the school leader has scheduled a meeting with you. He spoke with you earlier in the year regarding leaving your classroom unsupervised. You assume this will be the topic of your meeting.

1. After the school leader has stated the problem, you say, "I apologize for leaving the classroom. It won't happen again. However, I did want to talk with you about several of my students. I spoke with the guidance counselor and he feels like these students should have never been put in the same class together. Can we get their schedules changed?"

2. Shortly thereafter, you say, "Another problem I would like to discuss is my prep time. This is the second year in a row

when my prep time is at the end of the day. It does not do me any good to have prep time at the end of the day. I told you last year I needed my prep either early in the day or toward the middle of the day to help me stay organized. Why wasn't I given a better prep time?"

3. A little bit later, you say, "I hear what you are saying. Could we also talk about the number of copies I get each month? It is not nearly enough. Do you know I have to use another teacher's copy code and the local copy company to get copies for my classes? This is unacceptable. I can barely get by on my salary and now have to use my hard-earned money to pay for copies. Who do I see about getting more copies?"

4. Once an improvement plan is mentioned, you say, "Why didn't you tell me this was going to be about an improvement plan? I would have demanded my union representative be here."

Scenario 3

Role of School Leader

Your Language Arts teacher is also the sponsor for the play. You are told that the teacher has used profanity toward students on multiple occasions. You had heard this rumor last year. You are meeting to bring the concern to the teacher's attention.

Role of the Employee

You are a Language Arts teacher and a sponsor of the upcoming play. You assume the meeting will be about the fact that you have used profanity toward students during play practice.

1. At the beginning of the meeting, after the concern is brought to your attention, you say, "Come on, students talk worse

than I do on a daily basis. Do you see what they watch on their phones?"

2. Later in the meeting you state, "Our plays get rave reviews. How do you expect me to motivate students to be their best? You have to admit I do a great job."

3. Toward the end of the meeting, you say, "Okay, I will try not to use profanity, but I can't promise you anything."

Scenario 4

Role of School Leader

You are meeting with a teacher who is consistently late for work. However, yesterday he was so late that first period had already started, and students were seated and unsupervised in his classroom. You have voiced your concern with this employee in the past, but now feel you need to address the concern and develop an improvement plan.

Role of the Employee

You are a teacher who routinely arrives to work late. The school leader has requested a meeting and you assume it is because of your frequent tardiness to school.

1. As the school leader brings the concern to your attention, you state, "I admit I have been tardy lately, but I promise the behavior will change."

2. Then you state, "Haven't I done everything you have asked me to do? Every teacher has their areas of strengths and areas for growth. I plan to get better."

3. Later in the meeting, you state, "I think I am a very good teacher. I have admitted to being late and that I will remedy the problem. Can't this be the end of this issue?"

4. Toward the end of the meeting, you say, "I am struggling with this meeting. I plan to talk with the Association and see if they can do anything. Had I known what this meeting was about, I would have had an Association representative here with me. This meeting was unfair."

Scenario 5

Role of School Leader

You are meeting with a teacher who has a reputation for being extremely negative in the teacher's lounge. Recently, other staff members have shared with you that they feel like the teacher is having a negative impact on the culture of the school. You know this teacher is negative but have avoided confronting them about their negative behavior.

Role of the Employee

You are a veteran teacher who likes to hang out in the teacher's lounge and complain. The school leader has requested a meeting and you assume your teacher's lounge behavior will be the topic.

1. As the school leader brings the concern to your attention, you state, "You have got to be kidding me. Have you heard of this thing called free speech?"
2. Later, you state, "I have been teaching since the time you were in diapers. I have seen many so-called leaders, come and go, and guess who is still here?"
3. Later in the meeting, you state, "The real issue is your lack of leadership. This entire staff thinks this school is going in the wrong direction."
4. Toward the end of the meeting, you say, "I have no problem going to the school board and tell them of your attempts to

stifle my first amendment rights. I might even contact the local paper and share with them your Gestapo-like tactics."

CHAPTER SUMMARY

Practice makes perfect. A school leader can use role playing scenarios with a colleague, invite a third-party coach to observe practice facilitation, or record practicing confrontation facilitation skills and then review the recording to identify strengths or areas for improvement.

One of the most effective methods to help a school leader improve their facilitation skills is role playing. During role playing with a colleague, the person playing the role of an employee should try to deflect to the conversation by making various comments to distract the school leader.

This chapter includes five practice scenarios a school leader can use with a colleague to practice their Confrontation Management skills.

Chapter Six

Examples of Confrontational Conversations

The following pages include ten real-world scenarios that involved a school leader who had facilitated a confrontational conversation with a staff member. The leader has reflected on the conversation and shared their perspective on the confrontational conversation including their perception on whether the conversation went well, areas for improvement, and whether the relationship was positively or negatively impacted by the confrontational conversation.

EXAMPLE #1

High School Principal Meeting with Teacher

Issue or Concern

Social media postings were brought to the attention of a high school principal regarding a teacher who worked in his school. The teacher was posting pictures of a trip to an out-of-state amusement park, however the teacher had submitted sick leave for the duration of the trip. Additionally, during the course of the investigation, it was discovered that the teacher was using school property to operate a private business during business hours.

How Did the Meeting Begin?

"I began the meeting by sharing the concern regarding sick leave that coincided with pictures of the employee on vacation with family. I also brought up the concern about running a private business during school hours."

Employee reaction to concern

"First, the employee was in denial and shared a story about a sick boyfriend and some medical appointments for her children. When pressed, the teacher finally admitted to the fraudulent use of sick leave."

What did you do when the employee tried defending or deflecting?

"The employee tried several times early in the initial meeting to deny and deflect. I continued to request evidence of the claims, as I knew travel documentation would be easy to produce. The teacher was unable to provide the documentation I requested and that was very telling for me."

Reflection from meeting with employee

"I think I was able to ask straight forward questions and was able to take any emotion out of my side of the confrontation. The employee was obviously emotional so I didn't need to add to that situation."

What did not go well?

"It took longer to get to the truth than I would have liked. I am sure the employee felt I was being harsh as I continued to ask for the documentation and refused to allow her to continue to postpone getting the documentation."

Did the conversation have any impact on your relationship with the employee?

"Yes. The employee resigned and probably blames me for their resolution."

If you could have a "do over" is there anything you would do differently?

"No. Unfortunately, I think the situation needed to be resolved in the manner that it was handled. There was too much to overcome."

EXAMPLE #2

Superintendent Meeting with Athletic Director

Issue or Concern

"Our district was in the process of moving from a full-time high school athletic director to a middle school and high school activities director. As a result, the person who has served as our athletic director, and will be assuming the new role, was less than thrilled with the change. After notifying him of the change, I began to hear from others that he was making it known to both staff members and community members that he was being asked to do too much and that the results would not be good. I called him in to have a conversation about how he was handling the situation, particularly with his comments to others."

Employee reaction to the concern addressed at meeting

"There was no denial. In fact, when I said that I was aware that he was 'complaining' to others, both within the system and outside it, he replied, 'I wouldn't call it complaining. I would call it whining.' I believe he understood my concern, acknowledged it, and promised to end it."

Did the employee deny, defend, or deflect?

"There was some defending that occurred. He was still trying to convince me that the job was too big for one person to do effectively, and that he was making sure other staff members were aware that their expectations should not be too high."

What did you do when the employee tried defending or deflecting?

"I was not surprised by the response. It was consistent with what I had heard from him during a prior conversation that he and I had had. My reaction was to go back to that earlier conversation and talk through the items that he was concerned about, and why we were moving to make the change."

Reflection from meeting with employee

"I have learned that you have to individualize conversations based on the person you're speaking with. Some people (this case was an example) require the conversation to be very blunt and straightforward. I thought I had been so in a prior conversation, but apparently not direct enough. I made sure to do so this time and believe it is what was needed. And I think he appreciated my doing so."

What did not go well?

"Despite offering the rationale for the decision (again) he was still adamant that it was not appropriate. It's usually my goal to try to get others to see the value and reasons for such decisions and can usually do so. I'm not convinced that that happened in this situation."

Did the conversation have any impact on your relationship with the employee?

"I don't believe it impacted our relationship in a negative way. If anything, it may have made it stronger. I have experienced several times where employees may not agree with decisions, but very much appreciate the fact that someone is willing to make them and to do so directly and confidently. I'm certain that he respected my doing just that."

If you could have a "do over" is there anything you would do differently?

"The only thing I can think of is that I probably could have avoided this last conversation by being more direct during our earlier discussions."

EXAMPLE #3

High School Principal Meeting with a Teacher

Issue or Concern

"I had a special education teacher that was getting into power struggles with students. I knew I had to sit down with him and have a 'tough conversation.' The main issue was his lack of understanding during the situation and that his actions were making students' behavior worse. For example, instead of trying to de-escalate a situation where a student was upset, he would do and say things that would further agitate the student. Other students and staff in the building could see that this teacher's behavior was negatively impacting students, so I knew I had to sit down and talk with him."

Employee reaction to concern

"First, I have a good relationship with this employee so I knew that we could be honest and open during our conversation. I tried to anticipate how he would react and my thoughts were correct. He became tearful and quiet. Second, this employee was going through a lot outside of school. His wife had recently left him and filed for divorce. He also had an accident earlier in the year and was dealing with concussion symptoms and headaches. My observations of his reaction were that he knew this was an issue and that things outside of school were affecting him in the building."

Did the employee try to defend, deny, or deflect?

"The employee did not say much during the meeting. He listened to my views and did not disagree or argue with me. He did share with me the significant events outside of school that were bothering him and how that may have an impact on his work during the school day."

How did you react to defend, deflect, deny?

"I realized that this conversation was going to need two things. First, I needed to provide support for the challenges that were happening outside of school. Second, I needed to provide resources for how to de-escalate student situations. I had prepared some handouts and some step-by-step guides to work with kids in difficult situations. Ultimately, we talked about how kids respect adults. Respect is earned and the employee felt that students should just automatically respect him because of his position. However, we pointed to other examples where having a relationship with kids prior to any behavior event can pay off when behavior escalates."

Reflection from meeting with employee:

"I think the employee felt supported during our conversation and that he also needed to improve. I think I was able to provide some great resources for him to utilize with students."

What did not go well?

"I wish I had followed up better after the conversation. I need to do that at the beginning of the year to make sure the things we talked about have been implemented."

Did the conversation have any impact on your relationship with the employee?

"It showed that I cared about the employee and I think it strengthened the relationship. I observed an improvement with kids after we had our conversation."

If you could have a "do over" is there anything you would do differently?

"I should have probably put this in writing. However, because the teacher had significant things going on outside of school, I decided to just have a verbal conversation. Looking back, I should have written something in case this presents itself in the future."

EXAMPLE #4

Superintendent Meeting with a Teacher

Issue or Concern

"We had a teacher have a student take the teacher's car during the school day to run a few errands for the teacher because the teacher didn't think they had time to get to it until later in the day."

Employee reaction to concern

"The teacher initially tried to downplay the magnitude of the situation. She really didn't see it as that big of a deal."

Did the employee try to defend, deny, or deflect?

"She didn't deny anything, but she tried to deflect and then defended her decision to allow a student to use her car and credit card during the school day."

How did you react to defend, deflect, deny?

"I was a little surprised that she didn't think it was a big deal, but once we helped her realize all of the potential dangers, she finally admitted it wasn't a good choice."

Reflection from meeting with employee

"I never lost my cool during the conversation. Even as she tried to defend her decision, I was able to maintain a level of calmness that allowed us to get to a point in which she better understood why it wasn't a good idea."

What did not go well?

"I don't know if anything didn't go particularly well, but it always amazes me how people can rationalize any decision that they make even if it is clearly a poor one."

Did the conversation have any impact on your relationship with the employee?

"I didn't think at first it had too much of an impact. The relationship remained professional and we had positive interactions after the meeting. However, she has since resigned, so ultimately confronting the problem did impact our working relationship."

If you could have a "do over" is there anything you would do differently?

"I cannot think of how I could have handled the issue any better. The employee used really poor judgment and it played out eventually like we thought it should."

EXAMPLE #5

Curriculum Director Meeting with a Principal

Issue or Concern

"I had a concern with the principal who has been displaying a less than stellar attitude toward staff, other school leaders, and me. This was concerning because she is leading a big team of over one hundred staff."

Employee reaction to concern

"She reacted with anger. When I was sharing the conversation with her she listened and when the conversation was done, I asked her for her input. She immediately went to anger. She used her hands and they were shaking. I could tell she was very angry with me. I stayed very calm."

What did you do when the employee tried defending or deflecting?

"She went directly to deflection and turned the situation as my fault because I am not communicating enough with her. She displayed anger in her voice and in her actions toward me."

How did you react to defend, deflect, deny?

"I was surprisingly calm because this was the second time this year I had visited with her about her attitude. I listened for a while and then I kept trying to swing the conversation back to the real issue, her attitude. She was determined for me to hear her side and how it was my fault."

Reflection from meeting with employee

"I think having prepared for the meeting with a typed script for presenting my side of the story helped me keep control of the conversation when it would start to stray. I also liked that I told her the conversation was between the two of us and no one else would need to know unless she chose to share it."

What did not go well?

"I know I let the conversation last too long. We had dialogue for about an hour. She was also so angry that her arms/hands were shaking. I didn't like that display of anger and probably should have called her out on it and/or rescheduled the meeting."

Did the conversation have any impact on your relationship with the employee?

"I am not sure of the long-term impact of the conversation. I would say yes in one aspect as she had said she felt that I 'had changed' and I tried to explain that I am the same person. On the other hand,

I am guessing she felt my authoritative voice in our meeting and that may have confirmed some of her thinking."

If you could have a "do over" is there anything you would do differently?

"I accomplished what I need to with the meeting. The do over would have been letting her speak after my initial conversation and then wrapping up the meeting. I let it go on longer than necessary."

EXAMPLE #6

Director of Human Resources Meeting with School Leader and Direct Supervisor

Issue or Concern

The issue was a school leader who was unable to build relationships with others. Additionally, the school leader's immediate supervisor was unable to successfully communicate problems for improved results.

How did the meeting begin?

"I began the meeting by sharing that the school leader had very good technical knowledge, but was unable to build relationships with others. Further, I stated that she was not working from a coaching perspective but rather from a model of an expert who tells and yells."

Employee reaction to concern

"The employee was very defensive. Even when presented with examples, the employee continued to defend or deflect from her behavior."

Did the employee try to defend, deny, or deflect?

"I kept coming back to the main concern. Then I asked her to summarize my concerns. To my surprise, she missed the main concern."

Reflection from meeting with employee

"I think we had an honest conversation, shared concerns, expectations, and really made sure she understood the concerns. Her immediate supervisor and I addressed what success looked like, and what would happen if her performance did not improve."

What did not go well?

"I had the conversation with her direct supervisor present. It should have been the direct supervisor leading the conversation."

Did the conversation have any impact on your relationship with the employee?

"I am not sure. I was addressing an issue with hopes that she would make the necessary improvements. It wasn't personal."

If you could have a "do over" is there anything you would do differently?

"I would have the conversation sooner than I did. Her lack of relationships was clearly an issue, but we let it build up and it should have been addressed sooner for her sake, and for the sake of the organization."

EXAMPLE #7

Superintendent Meeting with Teacher

Issue or Concern

All certified employees had agreed to work a night duty as part of the bargaining agreement. A teacher refused to work a night duty taking tickets at a ball game.

Employee reaction to concern

"The employee stated that she had already given the district tons of time and her kids attend another district and she should not have to do this because it was not stated in her contract. Additionally, the teacher had earlier sent an email that was very confrontational regarding being asked to take tickets at one event."

Did the employee try to defend, deny, or deflect?

"She tried to defend her position by telling me that she has many night meetings as a preschool teacher."

How did you react to defend, deny, deflect tactics?

"I listened and took notes. I continued to ask questions to lead the employee to a spot where she could not defend her arguments any longer."

Reflection from meeting with employee

"I stayed calm and did not let the employee get me off subject. I was respectful but firm with my expectations. I ended the conversation by making sure the employee understood what was expected of her and that we would follow up if these changes don't occur. I asked the employee if she had any questions."

What did not go well?

"I thought the conversation went well."

If you could have a "do over" is there anything you would do differently?

"This type of conversation can cause me problems with my 'emotional triggers.' Having emotional intelligence training helped prevent me from getting mad and helped me to stay focused on the teacher's behavior."

EXAMPLE #8

Athletic Director Meeting with Coach

Issue or Concern

"A coach used derogatory language in addressing a player in front of the team. This was not the first time this issue was brought to my attention."

Employee reaction to concern

"The coach downplayed the situation as if he couldn't remember the incident clearly and then communicated that he used different language (that wasn't offensive) and that it was simply a misunderstanding."

Did the employee try to use defend, deflect, deny tactics?

"Yes, the employee used sarcasm, and communicated that the parents have been out to get him."

What did you do when the employee tried defending or deflecting?

"This was a common response as it wasn't the first time this employee's behavior needed to be addressed. I simply restated his position, made sure he knew that the situation needed to be taken seriously and that further investigating would be necessary."

Reflection from meeting with employee

"I was prepared as I had grown accustomed to dealing with this individual and his reaction was predictable."

What did not go well?

"During the initial communication, everything was handled appropriately; however, further investigation would reveal inaccuracies in testimony and the changing of the narrative."

If you could have a "do over" is there anything you would do differently?

"No. Most of the regret was that the employee's behavior wasn't addressed in the years prior in a manner that would have either prevented the situation or led to termination."

EXAMPLE #9

Director of Special Education Meeting with Teacher

Issue or Concern

"A special education teacher had not entered progress-monitoring data in a timely manner following a meeting in which the expectation was communicated. After doing a spot check approximately one week following the meeting, I realized the teacher had not yet followed through with this expectation of entering progress-monitoring data, so I left a voice mail with a request to comply. Three weeks following the voice mail, I did another check and realized progress monitoring had still not been entered. As such, I emailed the teacher to set up a meeting with the teacher and another supervisor present, in order to confront the employee."

Employee reaction to concern

"The employee shook his head in agreement and agreed to change his actions."

Did the employee try to use defend, deflect, deny tactics?

"No."

Reflection from meeting with employee

"I initially wanted to speak with the employee immediately following the realization the employee's work was not meeting expectations. Instead, I set up the meeting for a few days later, so the employee would have time to think about the potential outcomes of the meeting. The timeline put pressure on the employee during the time between the communication and the meeting itself. During the conversation, the expectations and historical communications were clearly laid out, which made for a black and white rationale for improvement."

What did not go well?

"The employee appeared to take on a 'compliance' mentality. Rather than progress monitoring for instructional purposes, he frequently shared with his colleagues and me his ability to meet deadlines. In other words, while compliance went up, effectiveness as an educator did not necessarily proportionally increase."

Did the conversation impact your relationship with the employee?

"The employee was very responsive to future communication and expectations laid out for him. He frequently checked in to see if he was performing up to expectations during the ensuing years."

If you could have a "do over" is there anything you would do differently?

"I would help the employee understand *why* progress monitoring should be completed rather than to merely meet my own expectation."

EXAMPLE #10

Teacher Leader Meeting with Another Teacher Leader

Issue or Concern

"The district has been doing a lot of work in literacy as part of our school improvement efforts. A Literacy Leadership Team meets monthly to do some research and learning ahead of the professional development we provide the rest of the teachers. As a team we have developed district beliefs for literacy instruction and have decided which instructional practices align to the beliefs. Teachers were encouraged to start learning and implementing these practices. Members of the leadership team were to be models during this time of transition. There was one teacher leader that was not on board with the efforts and seemed to be holding the team back at times. She was not using the instructional practices agreed on by the team. A conversation was necessary to share perspectives and move forward."

Employee reaction to concern

"Since I approached the situation in a way that helped her realize I cared and was seeking to understand her perspective, she was much more willing to problem solve to find a solution. I was upfront and honest about how the rest of the team was feeling and what might be at stake if something didn't change."

Did the employee try to use defend, deflect, deny tactics?

"At first she started to defend her actions and make excuses."

How did you react to defend, deflect, deny tactics?

"I redirected the conversation back to the real issue and restated my goal to resolve it together. I invited her to share ideas and decide next steps to reaching the goal."

Reflection from meeting with employee

"I believe she appreciated me giving her an opportunity to share her perspective. I also believe that in order to resolve the issue and move forward, planning the action steps collaboratively was necessary."

What did not go well?

"I tend to empathize too much at times. I started to back down a little mid-conversation, but I was able to refocus and continue problem solving."

Did the conversation impact your relationship with the employee?

"I feel it made the relationship stronger. The monthly meetings seemed to go better after that. It was like a weight lifted off our shoulders."

If you could have a "do over" is there anything you would do differently?

"I would confront her sooner rather than waiting until emotions were so high."

Chapter Seven

Closing

Serving in a leadership position can be an incredibly meaningful and rewarding experience. School leaders are fortunate that so many talented, hard-working, and caring people choose to be educators.

Unfortunately, when working with students, parents, and school staff, issues rarely have black and white answers or a specific policy to resolve an issue. A school leader consistently deals in shades of gray, which requires the leader to use his or her judgment.

Therefore, when people step into a school leader position, they should consistently reach out to other school leaders to help them process and consider multiple perspectives with the myriad complex issues awaiting their decision.

Good or bad, most community members know their school leader. The leaders who are perceived to be good are revered and oftentimes legends in their community.

Great leaders cultivate a positive culture that inspires students and staff members and leads a student-centered culture with high engagement.

Staff members choose to stay at schools with a great culture for their entire career. Additionally, teachers who appreciate their school culture will also actively recruit other great staff members to join the team.

When a school leader is perceived to be bad, the culture can be toxic, and students and staff do not feel valued.

Data also consistently indicate that while pockets of excellence may occur, poor leadership also negatively impacts student achievement and results in lower levels of student learning.

In every profession, there are times when a person in a leadership position must confront an employee regarding an issue or concern.

The planning steps outlined in this book are intended to help you plan and facilitate a confrontational conversation in a manner that demonstrates respect for the employee that will hopefully result in a continued trusting and positive relationship.

Additionally, the different tactics an employee may use to sabotage a confrontational conversation are identified. A school leader who is aware of the tactics and prepared for them is more likely to avoid falling victim to those tactics.

Nobody likes being confronted about perceived negative behavior or actions and it is natural for a person to feel the need to defend, deflect, or deny.

In order to get to improved performance, those tactics must be dealt with effectively in order to steer the conversation back to the main issue and coach the employee to desired behaviors and actions.

The best way to improve performance is practice. Chapter 5 includes several practice scenarios. A school leader should find a colleague and role play the scenarios. A school leader will improve with practice.

The book includes several real-life examples from school leaders and their experiences confronting employees. The examples include both strengths and areas for improvement from those experiences.

Anyone who has served in a leadership position and has confronted employees will readily admit past mistakes and learn from their experiences.

The Confrontation Management protocols outlined in this book are meant to help guide you in your journey to becoming a more effective facilitator of confrontational conversations while preserving a quality, trusting relationship with an employee.

A school leader who is willing to have confrontational conversations, even though they are not always going to be perfect, is a leader who is on their way to becoming a transformational leader.

Good luck in your journey!

Chapter Eight

Confrontation Management Template

PRIOR TO PLANNING A CONFRONTATIONAL CONVERSATION

A school leader should consider facilitating a confrontational conversation in the following situations:

- The school leader has an issue or concern with an employee that has not been effectively resolved using a coaching model.
- The school leader has an issue or concern and the employee does not appear to have the ability or willingness to make necessary improvements.
- The school leader has an issue or concern with an employee and the employee does not demonstrate any sense of urgency to improve in the identified area.

STEP 2

The school leader identifies what they want to achieve by having a confrontational conversation. The leader needs to have clarity around specific areas of improvement and be able to clearly define the desired state to the employee.

PART I. PLANNING THE CONVERSATION

Step 1: State the problem with clarity
Step 2: Invite the employee into the conversation and avoid allowing the meeting to be hijacked
Step 3: Share the desired outcome(s)
Step 4: Discuss the details of an improvement plan
Step 5: End the meeting with intention:

Agree on what will be shared with staff
Acknowledgment and validation

PART II. FACILITATING A CONFRONTATIONAL CONVERSATION

Step 1: Selecting the date, time, and location of the meeting
Step 2: Communicating the need to meet with the employee
Step 3: Executing the confrontational conversation
Step 4: Within forty-eight hours of the meeting, seek out employee for social conversation
Step 5: Recognize, praise, and celebrate!